The 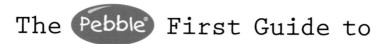 Pebble® First Guide to

Lizards

by Zachary Pitts

Consulting Editor: Gail Saunders-Smith, PhD

Consultant: The Staff of the Black Hills Reptile Gardens

Capstone press®

Mankato, Minnesota

Pebble Books are published by Capstone Press,
151 Good Counsel Drive, P.O. Box 669, Mankato, Minnesota 56002.
www.capstonepress.com

1 2 3 4 5 6 13 12 11 10 09 08

Library of Congress Cataloging-in-Publication Data
Pitts, Zachary.
    The pebble first guide to lizards / by Zachary Pitts.
    p. cm. — (Pebble books. Pebble first guides)
    Includes bibliographical references and index.
    ISBN-13: 978-1-4296-1710-9 (hardcover)
    ISBN-10: 1-4296-1710-1 (hardcover)
    ISBN-13: 978-1-4296-2804-4 (softcover pbk.)
    ISBN-10: 1-4296-2804-9 (softcover pbk.)
    1. Lizards — Juvenile literature. I. Title. II. Series.
QL666.L2P57 2009
597.95 — dc22   2008001398

Summary: A basic field guide format introduces 13 groups of lizards. Includes color
photographs and range maps.

Note to Parents and Teachers

The Pebble First Guides set supports science standards related
to life science. In a reference format, this book describes and
illustrates 13 groups of lizards. This book introduces early readers
to subject-specific vocabulary words, which are defined in the
Glossary section. Early readers may need assistance to read some
words and to use the Table of Contents, Glossary, Read More,
Internet Sites, and Index sections of the book.

Table of Contents

Cuban brown anole

Length: 8 to 16 inches (20 to 41 centimeters)

Eats: small insects, fruit

Lives: woodlands

Facts:
- flap at neck called a dewlap
- some can change color
- 340 species

Anole Range

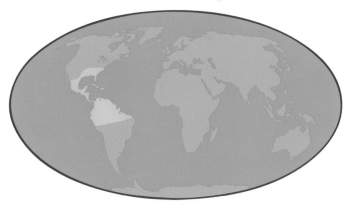

☐ North America, Central America, South America

green anole

Bearded Dragons

central bearded dragon

Length:	12 to 24 inches (30 to 61 centimeters)
Eats:	insects, small mammals and reptiles
Lives:	woodlands
Facts:	• has a spiky throat
	• able to wave to each other
	• 8 species

Bearded Dragon Range

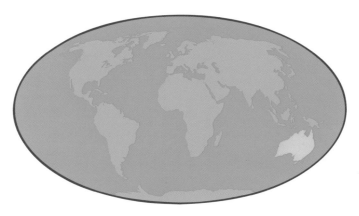

☐ Australia

eastern bearded dragon

Chameleons

carpet chameleon

Length:	12 to 24 inches (30 to 61 centimeters)
Eats:	insects, small lizards and birds
Lives:	woodlands, deserts
Facts:	• has a long, sticky tongue
	• can change color
	• 175 species

Chameleon Range

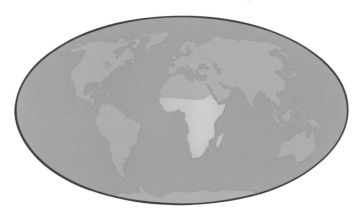

☐ central and southern Africa

panther chameleon

Flying Lizards

common flying lizard

Length:	8 to 18 inches (20 to 46 centimeters)
Eats:	tree ants, spiders
Lives:	woodlands
Facts:	• glide like a kite
	• can glide 100 feet (30 meters)
	• 28 species

Flying Lizard Range

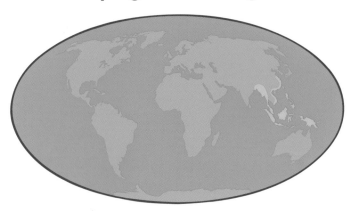

☐ southeast Asia

black-bearded flying lizard

Frilled Lizard

Length: 25 to 35 inches (64 to 89 centimeters)

Eats: insects, spiders

Lives: woodlands

Facts:
- skin on neck opens like an umbrella
- runs on two legs
- 1 species

Frilled Lizard Range

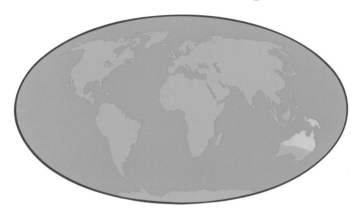

☐ New Guinea, Australia

Geckos

gold dust day gecko

Length:	3 to 7 inches (8 to 18 centimeters)
Eats:	insects, small mammals and reptiles
Lives:	rain forests, deserts, grasslands
Facts:	• licks own eyeballs
	• can walk upside down
	• 1,200 species

Gecko Range

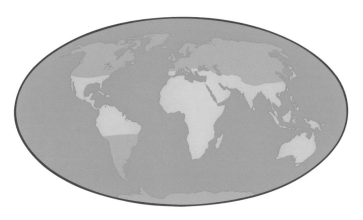

☐ all continents except Antarctica

Tokay gecko

Gila Monsters

Say It: HEE-la

banded Gila monster

Length:	19 to 24 inches (48 to 61 centimeters)
Eats:	bird and reptile eggs, small animals
Lives:	deserts
Facts:	• largest lizard in United States
	• have a venomous bite
	• 2 species

Gila Monster Range

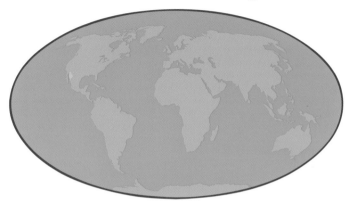

☐ southwestern United States, Mexico

reticulated Gila monster

Glass Lizards

eastern glass lizard

Length:	24 to 48 inches (61 to 122 centimeters)
Eats:	worms, snails, mice
Lives:	woodlands
Facts:	• look like snakes
	• tail easily breaks off
	• 15 species

Glass Lizard Range

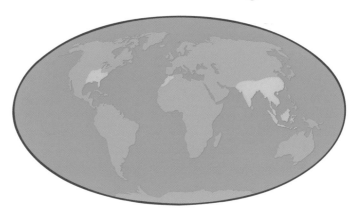

☐ North America, Africa, Asia

European glass lizard

Horned Lizards

short-horned lizard

Length:	3 to 6 inches (8 to 15 centimeters)
Eats:	ants, other small insects
Lives:	deserts
Facts:	• also called horny toads
	• able to spray blood from eyes
	• 14 species

Horned Lizard Range

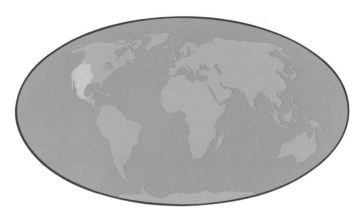

☐ North America

regal horned lizard

Iguanas

green iguana

Length:	36 to 78 inches (91 to 198 centimeters)
Eats:	leaves, fruit, insects
Lives:	deserts, rain forests
Facts:	• good swimmers
	• sometimes kept as pets
	• 37 species

22

Iguana Range

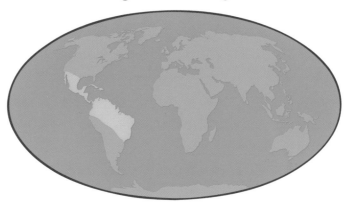

☐ North America, Central America, South America

Galápagos land iguana

marine iguana

Monitor Lizards

Komodo dragon

Length:	8 to 120 inches (20 to 305 centimeters
Eats:	insects, birds, reptiles, eggs
Lives:	deserts, rain forests
Facts:	• have a forked tongue
	• Komodo dragon is largest lizard
	• 86 species

Monitor Lizard Range

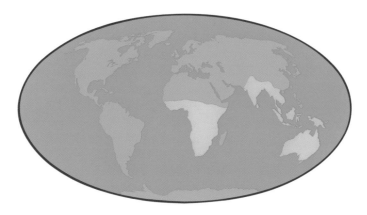

☐ Africa, Asia, Australia

quince monitor lizard

Skinks

western skink

Length:	5 to 16 inches (13 to 40 centimeters)
Eats:	insects, plants
Lives:	woodlands, deserts, grasslands
Facts:	• have smooth shiny scales
	• have very short legs
	• 1,200 species

Skink Range

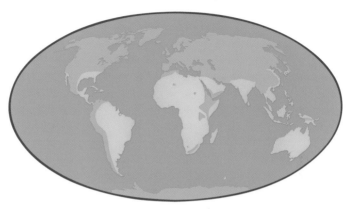

☐ North America, Central America, South America, Africa, Asia, Australia

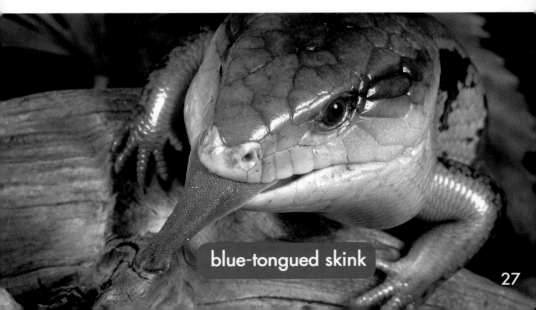

blue-tongued skink

Spiny Lizards

crevice spiny lizard

Length:	2 to 5 inches (5 to 13 centimeters)
Eats:	ants, beetles, spiders
Lives:	deserts, woodlands
Facts:	• good climbers
	• scales feel like a pinecone
	• 77 species

Spiny Lizard Range

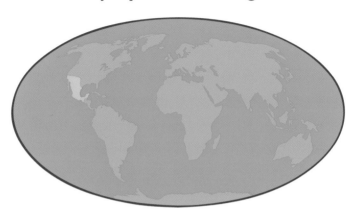

☐ North America

desert spiny lizard

Glossary

desert — a very dry area of land

glide — to move smoothly and easily

insect — a small animal with a hard outer shell, six legs, three body sections, and two antennas; most insects have wings.

mammal — a warm-blooded animal that has a backbone and feeds milk to its young.

reptile — a cold-blooded animal with a backbone

scale — one of the small hard plates that covers the body of a reptile

species — a group of animals with similar features; members of a species can mate and produce young.

venomous — having or producing a poison called venom

woodland — land that is covered by trees and shrubs

Read More

Bredeson, Carmen. *Fun Facts about Lizards!* I Like Reptiles and Amphibians! Berkeley, N.J.: Enslow, 2008.

Murray, Julie. *Lizards*. A Buddy Book. Animal Kingdom. Edina, Minn.: Abdo, 2005.

Internet Sites

FactHound offers a safe, fun way to find Internet sites related to this book. All of the sites on FactHound have been researched by our staff.

Here's how:

1. Visit *www.facthound.com*
2. Choose your grade level.
3. Type in this book ID **1429617101** for age-appropriate sites. You may also browse subjects by clicking on letters, or by clicking on pictures and words.
4. Click on the **Fetch It** button.

FactHound will fetch the best sites for you!

Index

Grade: 1
Early-Intervention Level: 24

Editorial Credits
Erika L. Shores, editor; Alison Thiele, designer; Danielle Ceminsky, map illustrator;
    Jo Miller, photo researcher

Photo Credits
Alamy/blickwinkel, 19
Bruce Coleman Inc./CB Frith, 10; Dwight R. Kuhn, 15; John Shaw, 12; Michael Fogden, 7
Getty Images Inc./The Image Bank/Bob Elsdale, 9; The Image Bank/Cousteau Society,
    23 (right); Stone/Tim Flach, 17
iStockphoto/James VanZetta, cover (gecko)
Nature Picture Library/Solvin Zankl, 11
Pete Carmichael, 4, 5, 8, 13, 14, 22, 27, 28
Peter Arnold/John Cancalosi, 16, 21
Photos.com, 26
Shutterstock/Amy K. Halucha, cover (bearded dragon); Hiroyuki Saita, cover (chameleon);
    Jason Speros, cover (iguana); Judy Crawford, 29; rebvt, 23 (left)
SuperStock Inc./ZSSD, 25
Visuals Unlimited/G. & C. Merker, 6; Jim Merli, 18; Joe McDonald, 20; Reinhard Dirscherl, 24